Get Started Selling on eBay in 2023

Basic Introduction Primer

by

Nick Panek

Introduction

If you're looking for a way to make some extra money, eBay can be a great platform to sell items online. With millions of users around the world, eBay provides a huge marketplace to reach potential buyers.

However, finding the right items to sell on eBay can be a challenge. You need to find items that are in demand and that you can sell for a profit. That's where research comes in. **RESEARCH IS THE MOST IMPORTANT STEP!!!!** It will save you from getting in over your head.

In this book, we'll guide you through the process of researching and finding items to sell on eBay. You'll learn where to look for items, how to determine their value, and how to identify profitable niches and categories. We'll also cover how to list items on eBay, including writing effective item titles and descriptions, taking and editing photos, and pricing strategies. Finally, we'll discuss shipping items and some risk management practices.

Before we dive into the specifics, it's important to understand the benefits of selling on eBay. One of the biggest advantages is the flexibility it offers. You can sell items from the comfort of your own home, and you can set your own hours. Additionally, eBay provides a huge audience of potential buyers, which can lead to higher profits than you might be able to achieve through other sales channels.

However, in order to succeed on eBay, you need to do your research. This means finding items that are in demand and that you can sell for a profit. By the end of this book, you'll have the knowledge and skills you need to start selling on eBay and to make your business a success.

While I can not guarantee success, I have personally had success using the following steps when I worked for a pawn shop as an eBay seller. I would note that fake YouTube gurus make wild claims these days about how great you can do on eBay and I just want to give perspective. Ebay, for all intents and purposes should be viewed as supplemental income, not primary, at least for most people. While it can be scaled up, there is often little reason to do so. I am going to be as realistic and honest as I can, unlike the cults of personality, as I have no personality (or so I have heard).

Chapter 2: Researching Items to Sell on eBay

One of the most important aspects of selling on eBay is researching the items you plan to sell. Doing your homework ahead of time can help you determine which items are likely to sell and how much you can reasonably expect to earn. Here are some key steps to follow when researching items to sell on eBay:

1. **Determine Your Niche (Or Don't).** Before you start looking for items to sell on eBay, it's a good idea to determine your niche. What types of products are you interested in selling? Are there certain categories that you know well or have experience in? By specializing in a particular niche, you can become an expert in that area and develop a reputation as a reliable seller. This is not necessarily essential, but it is very important if you decide to get into particular niches like precious metals, jewelry, collectibles, etc. I will expand on this later but for now if you just realize that there are many moving parts to specific

niches which may make you want to become an expert in those areas or avoid those niches altogether. I, for example, stay away from any car audio because in order to test them I would have to learn a whole new skill set that to me is not worth my time, but I have learned how to test gold and silver for authenticity and purity, as well as value.

2. **Look for Items in Your Local Area.** One of the easiest ways to find items to sell on eBay is to look for them in your local area. Check out garage sales, flea markets, thrift stores, and other local sources to find items that you can resell. This approach can be especially helpful if you're looking for unique or one-of-a-kind items that might not be readily available online. I will expand on this later, but this can be a very good way to source items to sell in some areas, while it isn't even worth the gas in others.

3. **Research Items Online.** If you're interested in selling a particular type of item, it's a good idea to

research it online to get a sense of what's popular and how much it's selling for. One great tool for this is eBay's completed listings feature, which allows you to see how much similar items have sold for in the past. Another way to use this method is to buy things wholesale in bulk. This makes it very easy to sell multiple copies of the same item without having to list each one, because if I have 50 pencil sharpeners I want to sell that are all the same make, model and color, I am only listing it once and just adjusting the quantity.

4. **Check Out eBay's Top Sellers.** Another way to get ideas for items to sell on eBay is to check out eBay's top sellers. These are the sellers who have the highest feedback ratings and the most successful sales histories. By looking at what these sellers are selling, you can get a sense of what's popular and what's in demand. This is something that is useful, but is by no means the only thing. In fact it isn't necessarily even essential until you want to expand.

5. **Attend Trade Shows and Conferences.** If you're serious about selling on eBay, it's worth considering attending trade shows and conferences related to your niche. These events can be a great way to connect with suppliers, learn about new products, and network with other sellers. This is useful in my local area in the precious metals niche as I can occasionally pick up Goldbacks, which are gold currency, for less than they sell for online. Other than something like that or to see if there is something new that you can possibly capitalize on, don't worry about this one.

By following these steps and doing your research, you can increase your chances of finding items to sell on eBay that are in demand and that you can sell for a profit. In the next chapter, we'll discuss how to list these items on eBay to attract buyers and maximize your sales.

So, let's say you are out and about at a garage sale

and you see a video game that they are selling for $5. How do you determine whether or not to buy it in order to resell it on eBay?

Chapter 3: Researching: How To

Researching the value of an item is a critical step when selling on eBay. Knowing how much similar items have sold for in the past can help you determine a reasonable price for your item and increase your chances of making a sale. Here are the steps to follow when researching the value of an item on eBay (I will follow up with a couple of specific examples):

1. **Search for the Item.** The first step is to search for the item you're interested in selling on eBay. Use a specific and detailed description of the item to narrow down your search results. For example, if you're selling a specific type of camera, include the brand, model number, and any notable features in your search query.

2. **Sort the Results by Completed Listings.** Once you've found your item, you'll want to sort the search results by completed listings. This will show you the items that have sold in the past, as well as those that didn't sell. To do this, check the

"Sold Items" box on the left-hand side of the search results page. This will filter the results to show only items that have sold.

3. **Analyze the Completed Listings.** Now that you've sorted the search results by completed listings, you can start analyzing them. Look at the items that have sold and note their final selling price. You can also look at the items that didn't sell and note their starting price and any other relevant details.

4. **Consider the Condition of the Items.** When analyzing completed listings, it's important to consider the condition of the items that sold. Items that are in good condition and come with all the original accessories and packaging will typically sell for more than those that are damaged or missing parts. Make sure to compare the condition of the items in the completed listings to the condition of the item you're selling.

5. **Look for Patterns.** As you analyze the completed listings, look for patterns in the selling prices. For

example, are there certain sellers or brands that consistently sell for higher prices? Are there specific features or variations that increase the value of the item? This information can help you determine a reasonable price for your item and identify any niches or categories that might be particularly profitable.

6. **Price Your Item Competitively.** Once you've completed your research, you can use the information you've gathered to price your item competitively. Make sure to set a price that's in line with what similar items have sold for in the past, taking into account the condition of your item and any other relevant factors.

So what does this look like in the real world? Well let's say I am at a local WalMart in the clearance section and find an Onn Premium USB Recording Microphone Model 100009002 on clearance for $7. I would start by typing that into the search bar on eBay, then I would hit the search button.

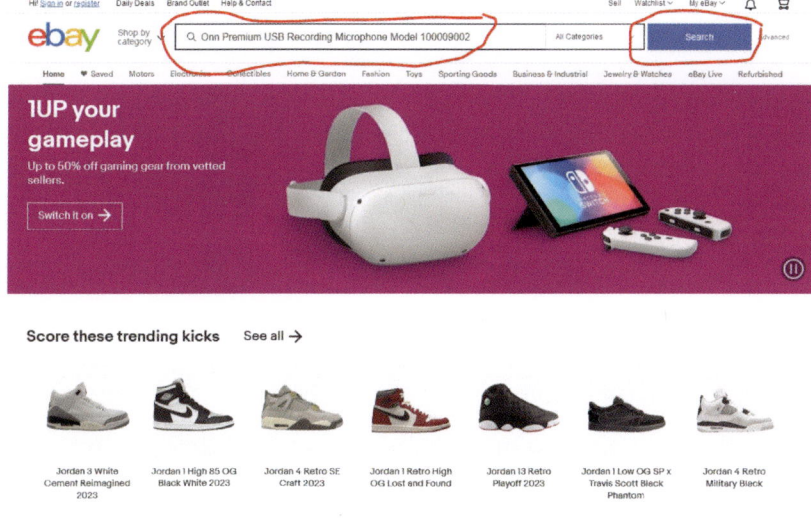

This will bring up a list of that item for sale on eBay currently.

Continued on Next Page

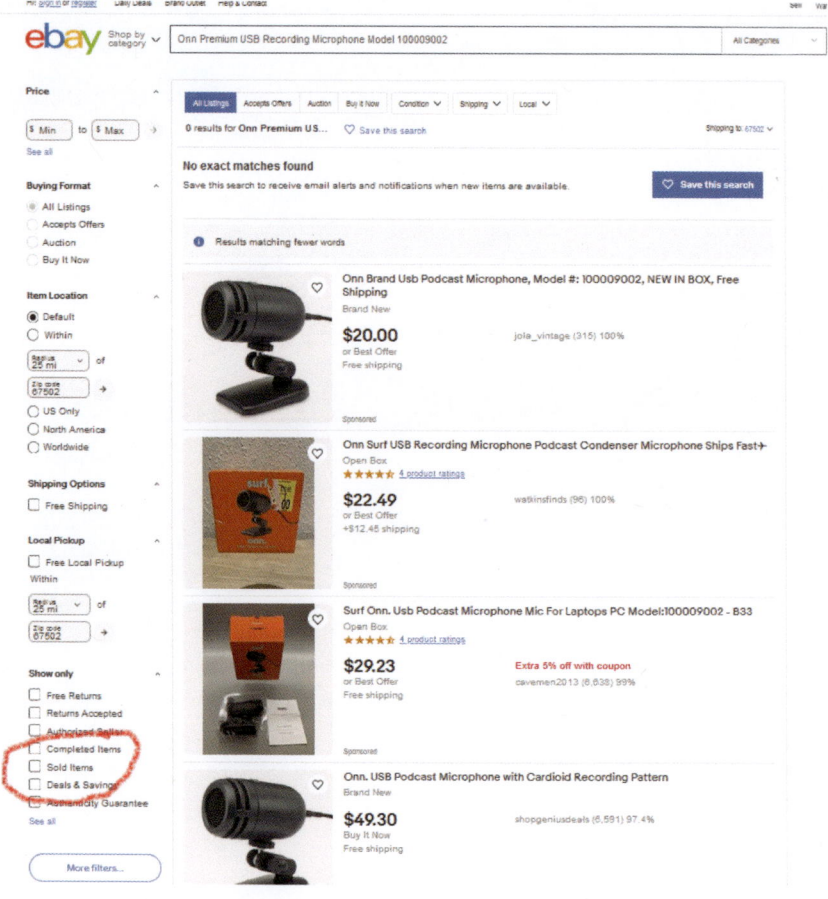

It is important to remember we are not done yet, these are just the prices people are asking for things not what they actually sell for. In order to find that information we must filter by Sold Items, which on the computer is on the left hand side, as shown circled in red above. On the phone, however, the filter is usually up top and depending on your device you may need to hit "Show More" to get to the Sold Items button. Once you click sold items, if it does not automatically change the page hit "Show Results" and you should see something similar to this:

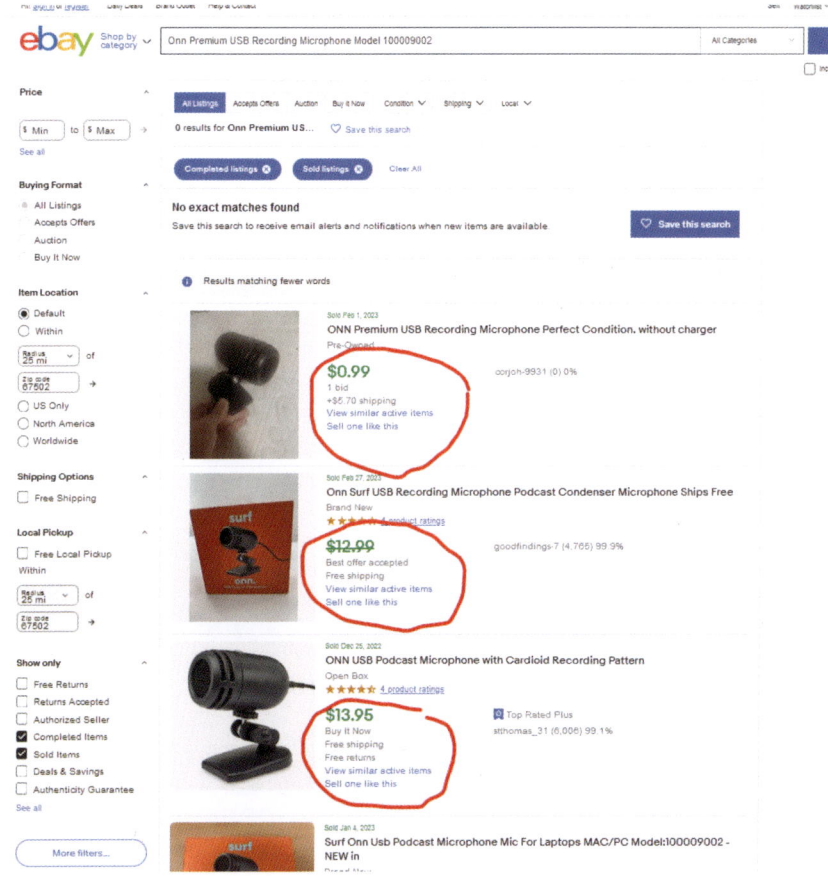

As you can see the prices are in green now. But there are a few things to look into. First of all, the first item shows that it only sold for $0.99and charged shipping and is used. The second one, with the line through the $12.99 offered free shipping and that line through the price means that they accepted an offer for a Brand New one. The third one, with the condition being open box, sold from a top rated seller for $13.95 with free shipping.

My personal analysis for this particular item at a price point of $7 would be no deal for me. If you offer free shipping that means you pay for the shipping which comes out of profits, plus the fees associated with eBay, and the time taken to list it would not be worth my time for a potential profit of mere pennies.

You can make your own decisions on what things are worth your time, but for me I like to, at bare minimum, double my money, and unless it is something that I can buy several of and do one listing I never waste my time for less than $20 in profit, though that may be going up soon due to the economy. That is just my personal preference. You will have to decide for yourself what your time is worth.

I will do another example.

Let's say I see at a garage sale that someone is selling a used Nintendo Switch game called "Legend of Zelda Links Awakening" with the case and they want $10. In this case I would type that in the search bar and search it, and filter by sold, which will bring this up:

Continued on Next Page

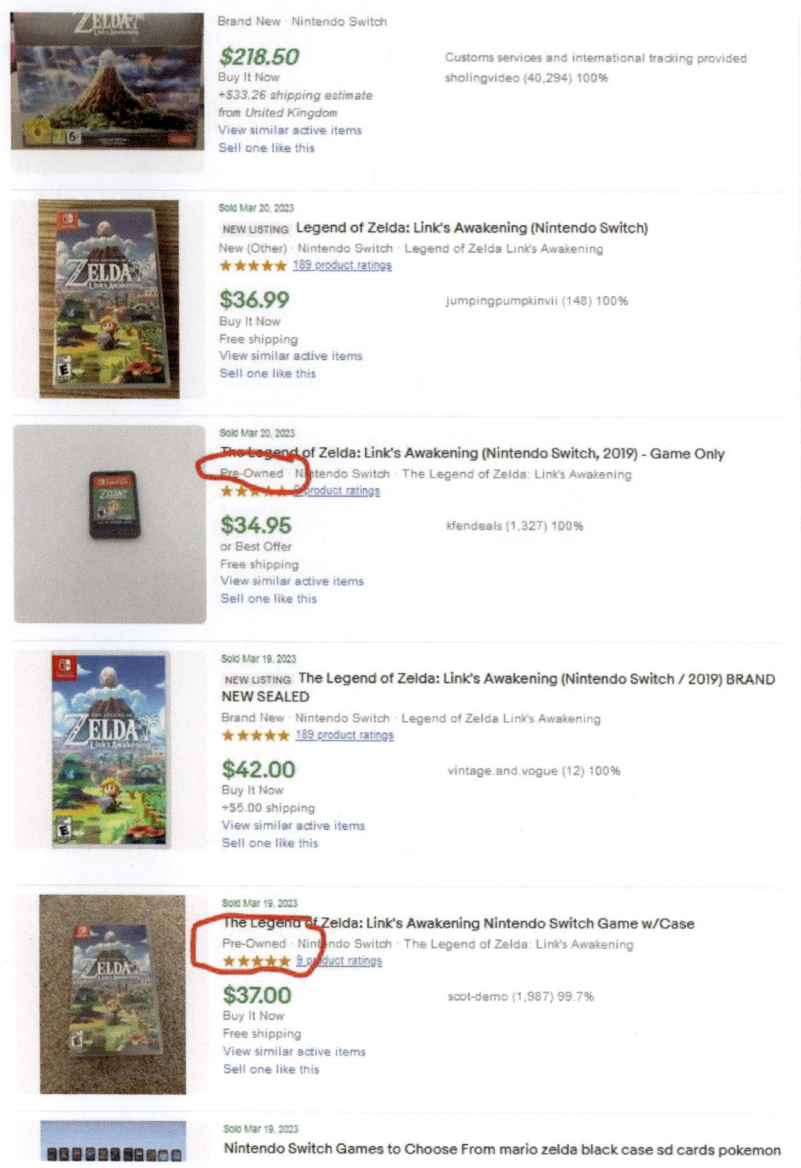

Now, the prices in green are the prices that they sold for. The 2 that I circled are the only ones that are in used condition and the second one has the case. So with this game I would buy it and expect to make about $20 after fees and shipping, so I would buy it. In fact with this being as small as it is and it can just be shipped via First Class through the Post Office in a bubble mailer I would probably buy it even if I only made like $10 because these are so easy to list.

    I recommend you try this with items around your house. Search them, sort by sold and see what may be worth listing.

Chapter 4: Listing Items on eBay

Once you've found items to sell on eBay, the next step is to create listings that will attract buyers and generate sales. Here are some key steps to follow when listing items on eBay:

1. **Set Up Your Seller Account.** Before you can start listing items on eBay, you'll need to set up a seller account. This process is relatively straightforward and involves providing eBay with some basic information about yourself and your business. Once your account is set up, you'll be able to create listings and start selling.

2. **Write Effective Item Titles and Descriptions.** One of the most important aspects of creating a successful eBay listing is writing effective item titles and descriptions. Your title should be clear and concise, and it should include keywords that buyers might use when searching for your item. Your description should provide all the information buyers need to make an informed purchase, including details about the item's

condition, size, and any flaws or defects. Whenever I am listing something, if I think it is in great condition, I only call it good condition. If it seems perfect I call it very good. I undersell the condition because if you use words like great or amazing condition remember that condition is subjective and people online are picky and fickle, and if their definition of amazing means perfect to them they may return it.

3. **Take and Edit High-Quality Photos.** Good photos can make a big difference when it comes to generating interest in your eBay listings. Make sure to take high-quality photos that show the item from multiple angles and in good lighting. If necessary, edit your photos to enhance their clarity and make the item look as appealing as possible. Also take them with a white background, not only does this look better but it is my understanding that this is the only way eBay can cross-promote on Google. I ALWAYS take close up pictures of any damage as a good practice.

4. **Choose a Pricing Strategy.** There are a variety of pricing strategies you can use when listing items on eBay. Some sellers prefer to use auction-style listings, where buyers bid on the item and the highest bidder wins. Others prefer fixed-price listings, where the seller sets a specific price for the item. You can also offer buyers the option to make an offer or negotiate the price. This is my preferred method, though it does sometimes get annoying getting multiple very low ball offers on an item and having to counteroffer or decline.

5. **Create a Compelling Listing.** To generate interest in your eBay listing, it's important to create a listing that stands out from the competition. This might involve adding extra details about the item, offering free shipping, or including a bonus item or special offer. The more compelling your listing, the more likely buyers will be to make a purchase. One way that I have done this in the past is to offer free shipping, because people love that, you just have to build the price of the shipping into the price you're

asking for it. Ebay also lets you give out offers, like buy 2 books get a 3rd of equal or lesser value free.

By following these steps and creating effective eBay listings, you can increase your chances of generating sales and growing your eBay business. In the next chapter, we'll discuss how to ship your eBay items to buyers, including choosing the right shipping methods and carriers, packaging items securely, and handling returns and refunds.

Chapter 5: Shipping Items on eBay

Once you've sold an item on eBay, the next step is to ship it to the buyer. Here are some key steps to follow when shipping items on eBay:

1. **Choose the Right Shipping Method and Carrier.** When shipping items on eBay, it's important to choose the right shipping method and carrier. Consider factors such as the item's size and weight, the buyer's location, and the desired delivery speed. You can use eBay's shipping calculator to estimate shipping costs and compare different carriers. As a rule of thumb I prefer to stick with smaller items less than a pound so that I can use First Class shipping, but obviously that is not always an option.

2. **Package Items Securely.** To ensure that your items arrive at their destination safely and in good condition, it's important to package them securely. Use sturdy boxes or padded envelopes and include any necessary packing materials, such as

bubble wrap or packing peanuts. Make sure the item is well-protected and won't move around inside the box during transit.

3. **Calculate Shipping Costs.** When listing items on eBay, it's important to accurately calculate shipping costs. Make sure to factor in the cost of shipping materials, as well as any fees charged by the carrier. Also I do not recommend adding handling fees, they are unnecessary and buyers hate them.

4. **Print Shipping Labels and Tracking Numbers.** To streamline the shipping process, you can print shipping labels and tracking numbers directly from eBay. This makes it easy to track the shipment and provides the buyer with a way to monitor the progress of their order. Also, I play it cautious and always take the package directly to the post office or FedEx or UPS and I get a receipt showing I dropped it off.

5. **Handle Returns and Refunds.** Inevitably, some buyers will want to return items or request

refunds. When this happens, it's important to handle the situation in a professional and timely manner. Make sure to have a clear return policy in place and communicate it clearly to buyers. If a buyer requests a return or refund, respond promptly and work to resolve the issue as quickly as possible. Also, this is one area that the scammers pop up. I once sold a new Ryobi saw to someone only for them to return it a week later saying that they couldn't get it to work. When they returned it it had been used a lot, so clearly they just needed it to build a patio then returned it, basically using eBay and me as a free tool rental program. I was told by eBay this is the cost of doing business.

By following these steps and shipping items on eBay in a professional and efficient manner, you can build a reputation as a reliable and trustworthy seller.

Chapter 6: Risks of Selling on eBay

While selling on eBay can be a great way to make money, there are also risks involved. It's important to be aware of these risks and take steps to mitigate them. Here are some of the key risks associated with selling on eBay:

1. **Fraudulent Buyers.** One of the biggest risks of selling on eBay is fraudulent buyers. These are buyers who use stolen credit cards, file false claims, or engage in other fraudulent activities to scam sellers. To protect yourself, make sure to use eBay's seller protections, such as seller protection policies and buyer requirements. You can also check a buyer's feedback history and contact eBay customer support if you suspect fraudulent activity. Whenever I get an offer I click on the persons username and at least tru to get a feel for what sort of feedback they leave others. If they leave a lot of negatives or it is a new account, I decline the offer.

2. **Non-Paying Buyers.** Another risk of selling on eBay is non-paying buyers. These are buyers who win an auction or make a purchase but then fail to pay for the item. To mitigate this risk, make sure to set clear payment policies and follow up with buyers who fail to pay. You can also use eBay's unpaid item assistant to automatically open a case against non-paying buyers.

3. **Shipping and Delivery Issues.** Shipping and delivery issues are another potential risk when selling on eBay. Items can be lost, damaged, or delayed during transit, which can lead to dissatisfied buyers and negative feedback. To mitigate this risk, make sure to use a reliable shipping carrier and package items securely. You can also purchase shipping insurance to protect yourself against lost or damaged items. I also add signature verification on anything valuable or anything going to an apartment. This mitigates the risk of a high priced item being delivered to the wrong address or in the case of apartments the customer having their item stolen by a neighbor.

4. **Negative Feedback.** Negative feedback from buyers can be damaging to your eBay reputation and can make it harder to sell items in the future. To minimize the risk of negative feedback, make sure to provide accurate descriptions and photos of your items, ship items promptly, and communicate clearly with buyers. If a buyer does leave negative feedback, try to work with them to resolve the issue and improve their experience.

By understanding the risks of selling on eBay and taking steps to mitigate them, you can protect yourself and build a successful eBay business.

Conclusion

Ebay is a great way to sell items, but you need to make sure when you do it that you are buying things that will actually make you profit and you have to know that you will make mistakes along the way. The important thing is to learn from those mistakes and adapt. It takes more time than people realize and that is why it is important to value your time and once you get practice you will learn to be efficient. Do some practice runs, where you find an item and research it and see how much after fees and shipping you make. Rule of thumb on fees is 10%.

Printed in Great Britain
by Amazon